Welcome to the galaxy of Year 3 Oxford Handwriting for Victoria!

Hello, my name is Sirius, and I am the brightest star in the night sky! I'm here to help you along the way ... in a *Sirius* kind of way!

My ticket to the Moon

Name: ______________________________

Age: __________ Class: __________

Birthday: ____________________

Teacher: ______________________________

My progress passport

You are travelling on a spaceship expedition around the galaxy.
Colour in the circles as you progress through the book.

Aa

I can print.

ok

I can do baseline and top exits.

ig

I can do drop-in joins.

na

I can connect drop-in joins to a, c, d, g and q.

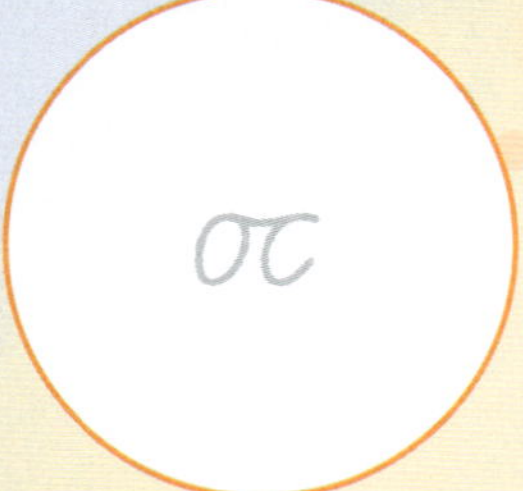

I remember to retrace for horizontal joins to anti-clockwise letters.

I can retrace horizontal joins to tall letters.

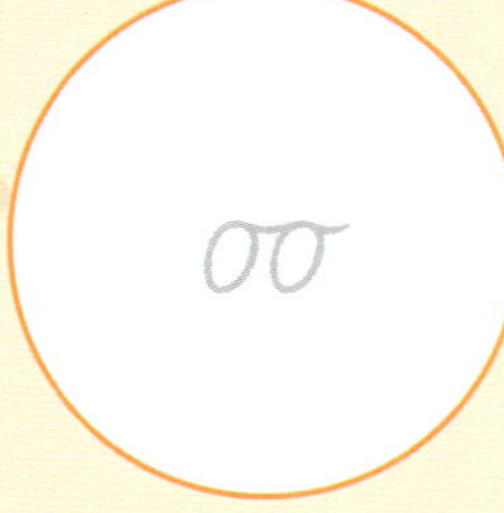

I can do horizontal joins to double letters.

I can do horizontal joins.

OXFORD UNIVERSITY PRESS

m

I can do entry and exit flicks.

qu

I can make a diagonal join from q.

if

I can join to f with a loop.

hi

I can do diagonal joins.

Blast off!

I can write fluently and legibly.

AB

I remember capital letters do not join.

bg

I know the letters g, j, y and z do not join.

Before you begin writing ...

Here are the 3Ps that will help you with your writing: **p**osture, **p**encil grip and **p**aper position. You will be reminded about these as you go through the book.

Posture

Relax your arms and make sure the chair supports your back. Put your feet flat on the floor.

Pencil grip

One of the most important decisions you can make is how you hold your pencil. Hold your pencil firmly between your thumb and index finger, balanced on your middle finger. (Your grip should be 2.5 centimetres before the end of the pencil. Don't grip too tightly!)

Left-handed

Right-handed

Paper position

Angle your page and use your non-writing hand to steady the page.

Left-handed

Right-handed

Left-handers may form some letters differently. For example, for the capital letters A, E, F, H and T, the left-handed person might go from right to left to make the join.

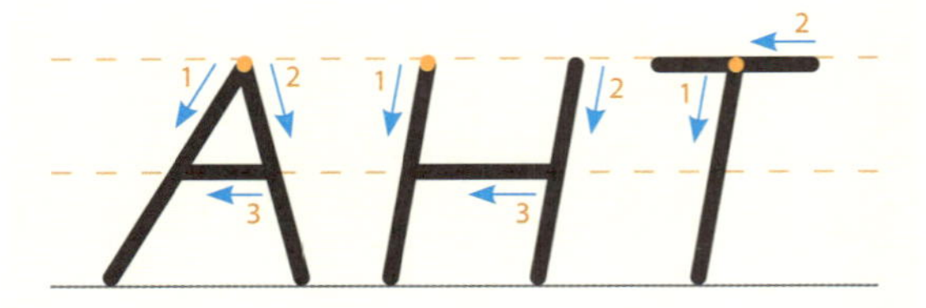

Revision

Victorian Modern Cursive print

Printing letters

Trace these lower-case and capital letters.

aA bB cC dD eE fF gG

hH iI jJ kK lL mM nN

oO pP qQ rR sS tT uU

vV wW xX yY zZ

Find and print all the tall lower-case letters that go into the "above" space. In the two boxes, print one letter that goes into the "above" section and the "below" section, and one letter that goes into the "above" section but does not reach the top dotted line.

above
on
below

b

Find and print all the short lower-case letters that fill the "on" section.

above
on
below

a c

above
on
below

Find and print all the tail lower-case letters that fill the "below" section.

above
on
below

g j

Printing numerals

Learning intention:

To revise numerals and punctuation using Victorian Modern Cursive print handwriting

Trace and then copy these numerals.

1 1 1 6 6 6

2 2 2 7 7 7

3 3 3 8 8 8

4 4 4 9 9 9

5 5 5 10 10 10

Printing punctuation

Trace and then copy these punctuation marks on the lines as shown.

. . . , , , ! ! !

' ' '

: : : ; ; ;

? ? ? " " / / /

Printing names

Learning intention:

To label diagrams using print handwriting

When we label maps and diagrams, we use print handwriting.

Neptune

Venus

Mars

Jupiter

Saturn

Uranus

Earth

Mercury

"My Very Educated Mother Just Served Us Noodles"

Match the name of the planet to the correct image and write it in the box in print handwriting.

Anti-clockwise patterns

Learning intention:
To practise letters with anti-clockwise patterns

Trace and then copy these anti-clockwise patterns.

Anti-clockwise

Trace and then copy these anti-clockwise letters.

a c d e f

g o q s

Write each anti-clockwise letter in the correct column. Write its capital letter next to it.

Short letters	Tall and tail letters
aA	gG

Clockwise patterns

Learning intention:
To practise letters with clockwise patterns

Trace and then copy these clockwise patterns.

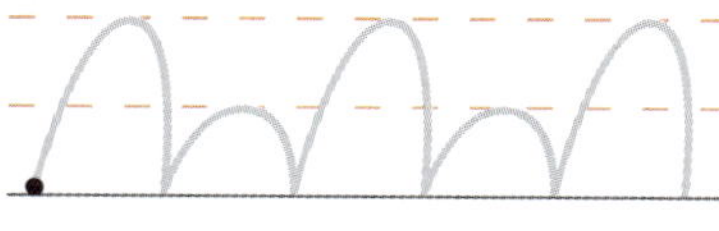

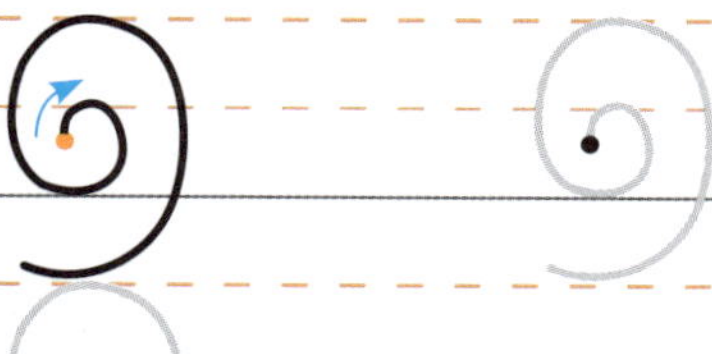

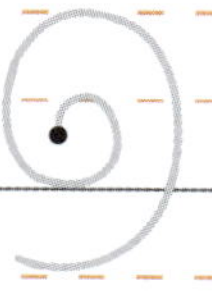

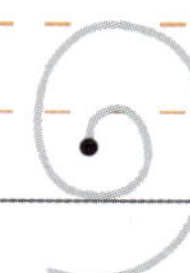

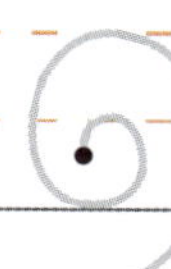

Trace and then copy these clockwise letters.

m n r h

p k x z

Complete the numbers on the clock. Then add an arrow to the grey line around the clock to show which way is clockwise.

What time is showing on this clock?

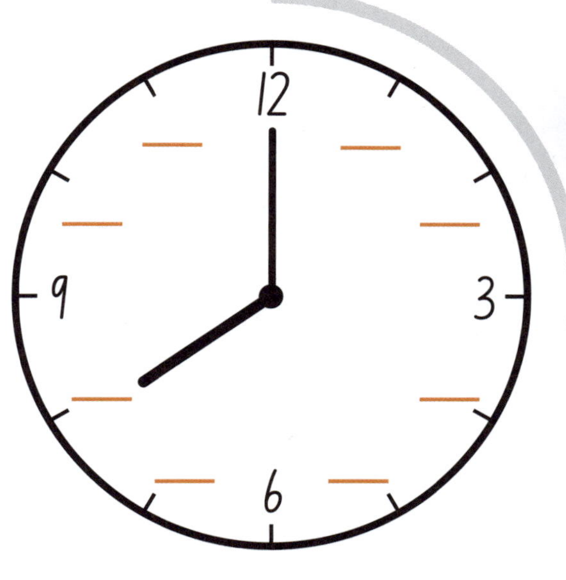

The letter x starts as a clockwise letter but the final stroke is anti-clockwise.

I-shaped patterns

Trace and then copy these i-shaped movements.

Trace and then copy these movements.

Trace and then copy these i-shaped letters.

l i t j

U-shaped patterns

Learning intention:

To practise letters that have a u shape

Trace and then copy these u-shaped movements.

Trace and then copy these u-shaped lower-case letters and capital letters.

b b b B B B

u u u U U U

v v v V V V

w w w W W W

y y y Y Y Y

Consolidating

Learning intention: To practise more patterns before writing

Trace and then copy.

Assessment: Print handwriting

Learning intention:

To combine all movements and write in print handwriting

Write all the capital and lower-case letters of the alphabet in print handwriting.

Aa Bb

Copy the following in print handwriting.

A day on Mercury is 1408 hours

and on Venus it is 5832 hours.

A day on Mars is 25 hours.

Self-assessment of print handwriting:

Congratulations! You have revised how to print. Colour in your progress on page 2.

- ❑ I need more confidence
- ❑ I understand but need practice
- ❑ Over the Moon!

Teacher comment

Passport

Anti-clockwise letters

Learning intention:
To practise letters with anti-clockwise movements

Remember that anti-clockwise letters go in the opposite direction to the hands of a clock.

Trace these anti-clockwise letters.

a c d e f g o q s

Anti-clockwise

Trace these anti-clockwise letters and words. Add the missing letters to complete the word.

a a a	constell _ tion
c c c	_ rater
d d d	asteroi _
e e e	m _ t _ or show _ r
f f f	_ ull moon
g g g	_ alaxy
o o o	techn _ l _ gy
q q q	_ uarter moon
s s s	_ upernova

OXFORD UNIVERSITY PRESS

Clockwise letters

Tip! Remember that clockwise letters go in the same direction as the hands of a clock.

Learning intention:
To practise letters with clockwise movements

Trace these clockwise letters.

h k m n p r x z

Trace these clockwise letters and words. Add the missing letters to complete the word. One of the missing letters at the start of a word is a capital letter. Do you know which one?

h h h	green _ouse
k k k	_uiper belt
m m m	co_et
n n n	u_iverse
p p p	Ne_tune
r r r	c_aters
x x x	space e_ploration
z z z	_odiac

I and u family letters

Remember that the letter t starts between the dotted thirds.

Learning intention:

To practise letters with i- and u-shaped letter movements

Trace these letters and words. Add the missing letters to complete the word. One of the missing letters at the start of a word is a capital letter. Do you know which one?

i i u u	_ n _ verse
j j j	_ upiter
l l l	ec _ ipse
t t t	spacesuit: space s _ a _ ion
b b b	or _ it
w w w	d _ arf planet
y y y	Milk _ Wa _
l l l	sate _ _ ite
u u u	astrona _ t

Baseline exits

Learning intention:
To curve and flick when a letter finishes on the baseline

I am successful when I can:
- ❑ check my 3Ps
- ❑ make my exit flick curved rather than pointy.

Trace and copy to practise your baseline exits.

a c d e h i k l m n p t u x

There are thousands and

thousands of asteroids. Most

asteroids are located between

Mars and Jupiter.

Small, rocky asteroids orbit the Sun.

Top exits

Learning intention:
To touch the mid-line then add a flick when a letter finishes on the mid-line

Trace and copy to practise your top exits.

b b o o

r r v v

w w

Copy this sentence on the lines below.

The brave astronaut waved goodbye to Earth as she rocketed towards the Moon.

I am successful when I can:
- ❑ sit with my back straight
- ❑ hold the pencil correctly
- ❑ position my paper.

Assessment: Baseline exits and top exits

Write four letters with baseline exits and four letters with top exits.

I am successful when I can:
- ❑ sit with my back straight
- ❑ hold my pencil correctly
- ❑ position my paper.

Trace and then copy this text.

Ravi the astronaut flew to

space in a speedy rocket.

Self-assessment of exits:

Congratulations! You've learnt how to do baseline and top exits. Colour in your progress on page 2.

❑ I need more confidence ❑ I understand but need practice ❑ Over the Moon!

Passport

Teacher comment

Letters without entry or exit flicks

Capital letters do not have an entry or exit flick because they don't join to other letters.

Learning intention: To understand that capital letters do not join to other letters

Trace and then copy.

Claudia and Ali went on a

mission to Jupiter, the fifth

planet from the Sun. They also

visited some other planets, and

saw asteroids and comets.

Entry flicks

Learning intention:
To understand that entry flicks are smooth

Entry flicks are small joins before a letter.

r

Trace and then copy the words below.

change pattern time natural

human actions erosion source

energy orbit night season

axis day galaxy dwarf planet

Circle your neatest word and tick three of your best entry flicks.

Consolidating

Learning intention: To neatly use letter entries and exits

Trace and then copy.

Sirius and Juliette loved

travelling to space in a rocket.

The absence of gravity made

them feel as light as a feather.

It was like floating through

a mystical, untouched world.

(Gravity is a force that holds

you to Earth's surface.) For years

it was believed that Earth was

the only planet with water.

NASA found evidence of

intermittent running water

on Mars too.

Using punctuation

Learning intention:
To practise writing punctuation

Trace and then copy the following text on the lines below.

Alessia read an amazing book

from her school library that

said: "In 1969, Neil Armstrong

became the first astronaut to

walk on the Moon".

I am successful when I can:

- ☐ check my 3Ps
- ☐ use punctuation.

Consolidating

Learning intention:

To practise writing letters with entry and exit flicks

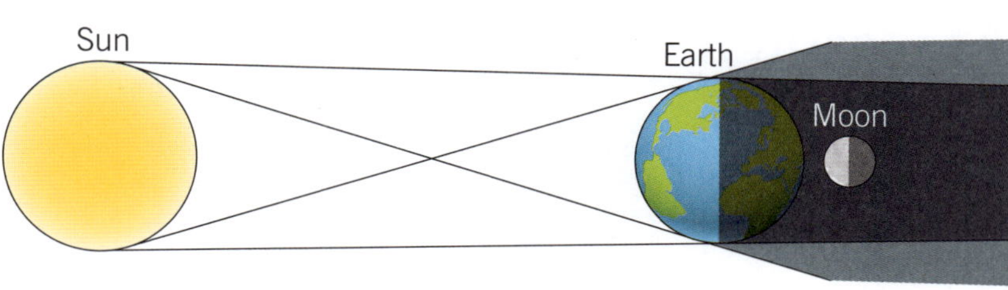

The Earth rotates on its axis every 24 hours, which makes day and night.

Trace and then copy the following text.

The Sun is a major source of

energy that warms our planet.

It takes the Earth and Moon

365 days (one year) to orbit

(to move around) the Sun.

Self-assessment *Draw a star on three of your neatest letters.*

Assessment: Entry and exit flicks

Trace and then copy these letters with baseline exits.

a c d e h i k l m n p t u x

Trace and then copy these letters with top exits.

b b o o r r v v w w

Copy these words on the lines below.

Earth planets galaxy Neptune

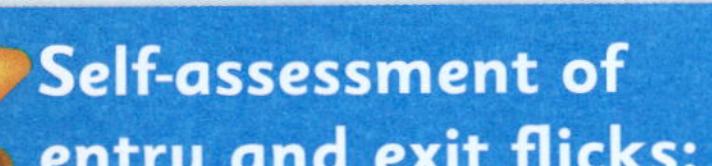

Self-assessment of entry and exit flicks:

Congratulations! You've learnt how to do entries and exits.

Colour in your progress on page 3.

- ☐ I need more confidence
- ☐ I understand but need practice
- ☐ Over the Moon!

Passport

Teacher comment

Diagonal joins

Learning intention:
To write letters with a diagonal join

Introducing diagonal joins

Let's warm up with some patterns first.

Now you're ready to join some letters. Practise the diagonal join first. This join links the exit and entry flicks between letters.

Trace and then copy these diagonal joins.

ai am an ap ar au ay

ce cu cy de di du dy

en em ei ey he hi hu

ay ce di ev in le tr

Practising diagonal joins

Learning intention:
To connect letters with a diagonal join

Can you continue the pattern without lifting your pencil?

uuuuu uuuuu

uuuuu uuuuu

ie → ie

Tip! The letter e changes shape slightly for a diagonal join to e. The letter s changes after a diagonal join. This shorter s means there is less to retrace, which will make your writing faster.

Trace and then copy these diagonal joins. The first one is done for you.

ie ip ki lm lu mp

ie

is → is

as is ds es hs ls

me ms pe ps ke ks

Trace and then copy.

ni ne nn nr nu py

te ti tn tr tu ex xi

ue ui um un up uy

exit tip in bin he pin him

Diagonal joins to tall letters

Learning intention:
To use a diagonal join to tall letters

Without lifting the pencil, you can make a diagonal join with an extended exit flick.

lower-case a — a with a diagonal line up — a joined to h

a a/ ah

Trace these diagonal joins to tall letters, and then copy them below. The first one is done for you.

ah ah ah ah al al al al

ah

ak ak ak ak ab ab xt xl

ch ch ch ck ck ck pt pl ph

Continue the pattern without lifting your pencil. Then go back and dot each letter i.

ilili ilili

this ✓ at   not this ✗ aʌt

Trace and then copy on the lines below.

at at at at at at at

it it it it it it it

ut ut ut ut et et et et

Let's look at double letters, for example, double t.

Trace and then copy.

tt tt tt tt tt tt tt

Matthew Garrett Wyatt Odette

Practising diagonal joins from q

Learning intention: To connect q with a diagonal join

The diagonal join from q to u is very long. Take the exit line from the q all the way to the top of the u.

Trace and then copy these letters.

q q q q q q

qu qu qu qu qu

Trace and then copy these words.

quiet quiz quest quip

quell quietly quiver

Some of these words might be new to you. Look up the definition, and write it on these lines.

Joining to f

Learning intention: *To join to f with a loop and lowered crossbar*

When joining to f, we add a loop at the top and sweep down to cross over at the mid-line and travel to the bottom of the tail space. Then we lift the pencil or pen and add the crossbar below the mid-line.

Trace and then copy.

af af af ef ef ef

if

if if if uf uf uf

often lift thief after

chief fifth offer nifty

Consolidating

Learning intention: To put diagonal joins into practice

Trace and then copy the following text.

The book "Hidden Figures" is about

three women, named Mary

Jackson, Katherine Johnson and

Dorothy Vaughan. They overcame

many obstacles to contribute to

the success of early space missions.

Assessment: Diagonal joins

Use a coloured pencil to make diagonal joins between these letters.

at it hi hu em ie

ke le me ni pr

Copy these diagonal joins.

ai hu ce im kn if af qu

Copy these words with diagonal joins.

little all aunty like then exit

Self-assessment of diagonal joins:

Congratulations! You have completed your diagonal joins. Colour in your progress on page 3.

❑ I need more confidence

❑ I understand but need practice

❑ Over the Moon!

Teacher comment

Drop-in joins

Introducing drop-in joins

Learning intention:
To write letters that contain a drop-in join: a, c, d, g and q

A drop-in join is used when we join to anti-clockwise letters. The exit flick from the first letter reaches high towards the top of the anti-clockwise letter. The anti-clockwise letter is dropped into place.

na

Trace and then copy these drop-in joins.

ma ic ed ng aq

ca da ea ha ia la na

ec id lc uc ad dd eq

Trace and then copy these words with drop-in joins.

quarter lunar giant name

Practising drop-in joins

Learning intention: To join letters with drop-in joins

The dropped-in letter should touch the high exit as it moves down. Make sure there is no gap between them (retrace where necessary)!

Trace and then copy the dropped-in letters. In another colour, draw a star where the letters meet.

ag dg eg lg ng ug da

ag

co aq eq ha iq ta ma

Trace and then copy these words with dropped-in letters.

again magic played night

aqua slack place jumped

eight equal star titan

Consolidating

Learning intention: To put drop-in joins into practice

Now you are ready to take off and write more connected words.

Trace and then copy these drop-in joins.

crunch aquatic lame staff

swimming leaf flag legend

accident happiness space travel

Trace and then copy.

seat standard came lunch screech

seal site star

titan small

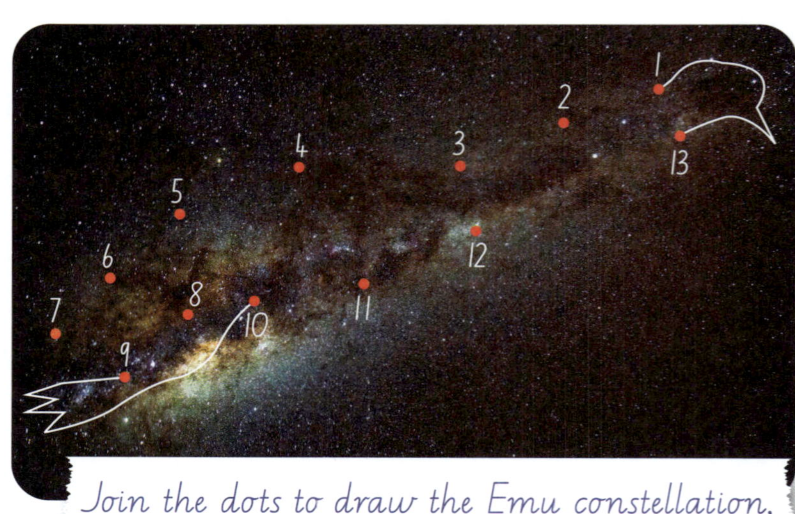

Join the dots to draw the Emu constellation, which is part of the Milky Way.

Assessment: Drop-in joins

I am successful when I can:
- ❑ check my 3Ps
- ❑ connect my letters in words.

Trace and then copy.

dad had lad mad pad

hug dig jig wig zigzag

bug big Tuesday right

helped happy play

Teacher comment

Self-assessment of drop-in joins:

Congratulations! You have completed your drop-in joins.

Colour in your progress on page 2.

- ❑ I need more confidence
- ❑ I understand but need practice
- ❑ Over the Moon!

Horizontal joins

Introducing horizontal joins

Learning intention:
To make horizontal joins

Tip! The letters b, o, r, v and w finish at the top of the letter, so we need to connect these letters with a horizontal join.

Continue the fluency pattern.

vuvw vuvw

Trace and then copy these horizontal joins.

bi br bu oi om on op or ou ov oy

ri rm rn rp rr ru rv ry

vi vu vv vy wi wu wv wy

Practising horizontal joins

Learning intention:
To join letters with horizontal joins

Copy these sentences. Then circle the words that contain a horizontal join.

Patrick loves to study the universe.

This morning, he won an award

for writing about asteroids. His

friends Lea and Jana won a prize

for finding the most constellations

when they were at camp.

Horizontal joins to anti-clockwise letters

Learning intention:

To join letters to anti-clockwise letters

retrace section

ra

When making a horizontal join to an anti-clockwise letter, go across to the start of the letter, then retrace.

The orange line shows where the letter is retraced.

oa oc oo og os od

Trace and then copy these horizontal joins to anti-clockwise letters.

ba bo oa oc oo og os od

oa oc oo ra rc ro rg rs rd

wa wc wo wg ws wd va vo

ocean Saturday

Did you know that Saturday was named by the Romans after the planet Saturn?

The letter d is the only tall letter that does not start at the top.
The horizontal join goes across to the starting point of the letter d.

od

Trace and then copy these words with horizontal joins to anti-clockwise letters.

today road excited rocket wow

voice garden core water

Write a sentence using the words above, and share your sentence with a classmate. Colour in the anti-clockwise letter pairs that you have in your sentence.

I hope you have fun using your imagination to come up with a sentence.

Write down your own anti-clockwise letter pairs.

Horizontal joins to tall letters

Learning intention:
To join letters to tall letters

When you make a horizontal join to tall letters, go right to the top and then retrace a little as you move downwards.

Trace these joins to tall letters.

ol rt rk wb wh ok

Trace and then copy.

ol ob oh ol ok

rl rk rh rb wk

wh wl wb vl vh

Trace and then copy these words.

chocolate girl bark stark when

woke solar white herbal orb

Horizontal joins to e

Learning intention: *To join an e horizontally*

For horizontal joins to e, dip even lower than other horizontal joins.

Trace the track of the shooting stars, using the dot as a starting point.

Trace and then copy the horizontal joins.

we ve re oe be

Trace and then copy the following words.

flower globe above active poem

tiptoe cobweb beam begins

revolve answer re-entry probe

Horizontal joins to and from f

Learning intention:
To join letters to and from f

For horizontal joins from f, join from the crossbar that slopes up.

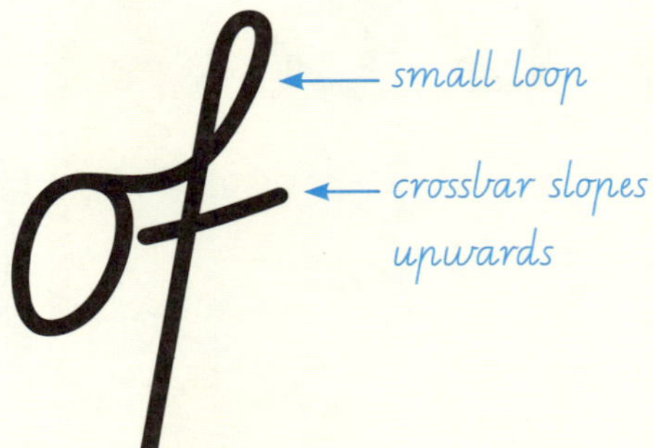

fe
lower crossbar join to e

Trace and then copy.

of rf wf fr fu fi fr fu fl fe

surf feel from flight funny

When f joins to an a or o, you need to retrace a little.

fa

Trace and then copy these horizontal joins from f to anti-clockwise letters.

found favourite family forty

Horizontal joins with double letters

Learning intention:
To write words with double letters

When we write double letters for b, f, o and r, we use a horizontal join. Make sure the double letters are not too far apart.

Trace and then copy.

bb ff oo rr bb oo rr ff

off offer foot waffle borrow

Practise your cursive handwriting by tracing this sentence.

Sirius is efficient with his current studies about outer space.

Consolidating

Learning intention:
To put my horizontal joins into practice

Trace and then copy.

My favourite friend is Finny.

Once, we went to the park with

my family at night. We looked

through a telescope and saw the

Moon. It was amazing!

Assessment: Horizontal joins

I am successful when I can:
- ❑ check my 3Ps
- ❑ write my letters with horizontal joins.

Copy these words with horizontal joins from b, o, r, v and w.

open town balloon array movie

Copy these words with horizontal joins to anti-clockwise letters.

wait wrong room cosmic rode

Copy these words with horizontal joins to short and tall letters.

start pool solar crater robot

Copy these words with horizontal joins to and from f and t.

family football fluff roof rotate

Self-assessment of horizontal joins:

Congratulations! You have completed your horizontal joins. Colour in your progress on page 2.

- ❑ I need more confidence
- ❑ I understand but need practice
- ❑ Over the Moon!

Teacher comment

Passport

Letters that do not join

Learning intention:
To write letters that have clockwise finishers: g, j, y and z

Introducing clockwise finishers

Trace over the following letters. Draw a star ★ to show where the letter ends. Draw an arrow to show the direction your pencil is heading in as you finish the letter.

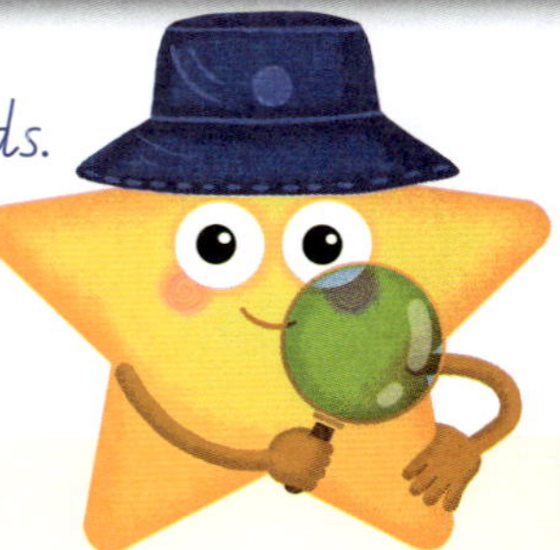

g j y z

Tip! Letters that finish in a clockwise direction below the baseline do not join.

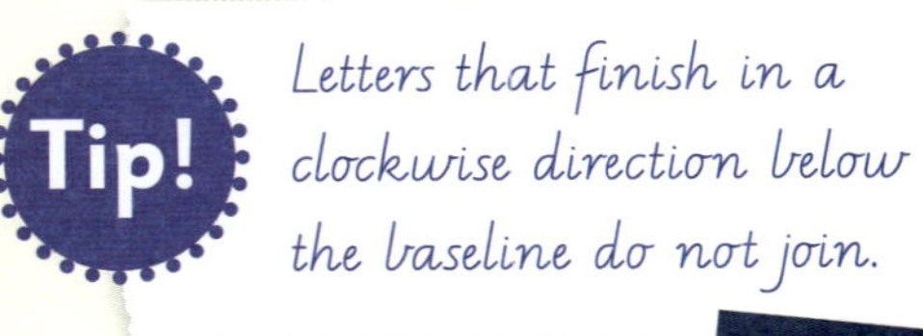

Passport

Trace and then copy.

g j y z

ge get gi digital go gone

gh bought ju just ja jam

ji jig yo you yu yum

zo zoom zi zip oz ozone

Voyager 2 is a space probe that

NASA launched in 1977 to zoom

around our solar system and

study Jupiter, Saturn, Uranus

and Neptune. It is still in space

zipping past planets.

Capitals

Learning intention: To write capital letters

Trace and then copy these names.

Ananya Henry Moon Binh

Emma Sirius Adam Hoa Ethan

South Pole Nico Charlie Natalia

Answer these questions on the lines below.

In which month were you born?	In which country were you born?	On which planet were you born?

Draw an arrow on the world map to show where you were born.

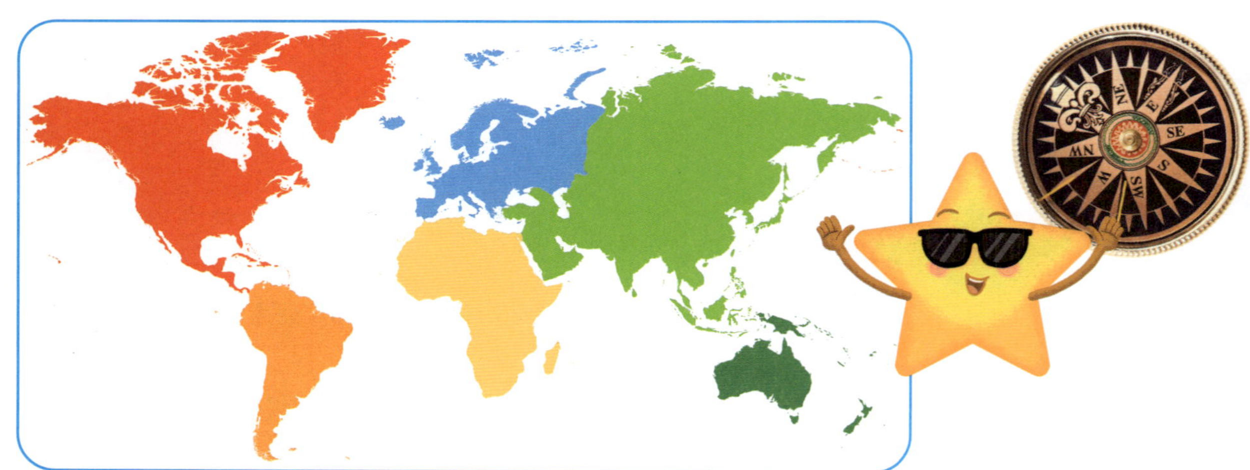

Assessment: Letters that do not join

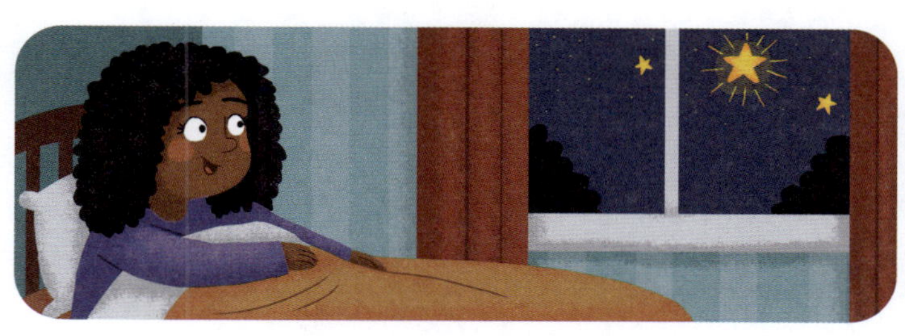

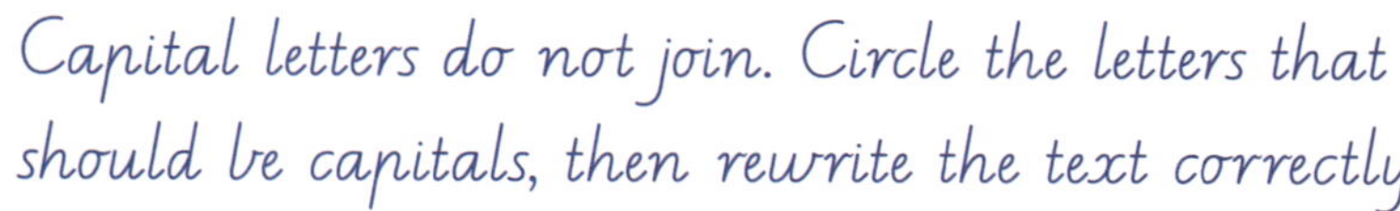

Capital letters do not join. Circle the letters that should be capitals, then rewrite the text correctly.

one night, juliette woke up and

saw a bright light in the sky.

she knew it wasn't the morning.

then she remembered that

sirius is the brightest star.

Self-assessment of letters that do not join:

Congratulations! You've learnt about letters that do not join. Colour in your progress on page 3.

❑ I need more confidence

❑ I understand but need practice

❑ Over the Moon!

Teacher comment

Fluency and legibility

Learning intention:
To practise cursive handwriting

Practising cursive handwriting

Trace and then copy these sentences.

A star is a hot, glowing ball of

gas. When you look into the

night sky, you can see stars.

During the day, our light

comes from the

closest star: the Sun.

Rewrite the information in these fact files in cursive handwriting.

Mars is red and is the fourth planet from the Sun.

Neptune is blue and is the eighth planet from the Sun.

Saturn has rings and is the sixth planet from the Sun.

The Kuiper belt has asteroids and dwarf planets.

Kuiper belt

Do you know how to pronounce Kuiper? You say KIGH-puh.

Size, slope and spacing

Rewrite the text, keeping in mind the size, slope and spacing of your writing.

Tip! Use your finger between words to make an even space.

this ✓

solar system

not this ✗

solarsystem

The solar system is named after the Sun. The word "sol" means sun in Latin. All the planets in the solar system revolve around the Sun.

Numbers

Trace and then copy these numbers.

1 2 3 4 5 6 7 8 9 10

10 20 30 40 50 60 70 80 90 100

Write these numbers as words on each line. The first one is done for you.

11 eleven eleven eleven eleven

12 twelve

15 fifteen

17 seventeen

18 eighteen

19 nineteen

20 twenty

21 twenty-one

Punctuation

Trace and then copy these punctuation marks and their names.

. . . full stop , , , comma

! ! ! exclamation mark ! ! !

? ? ? question mark ? ? ?

“ ” speech marks “ ”

Copy these sentences and choose the right punctuation mark to go at the end of each sentence.

Space travel is amazing

Do you have a favourite planet

OXFORD UNIVERSITY PRESS

Labelling maps and diagrams

Learning intention:
Use print handwriting for labels

Complete the state and territory names on the map of Australia.

Tip! We use Victorian Modern Cursive print handwriting to label maps and diagrams.

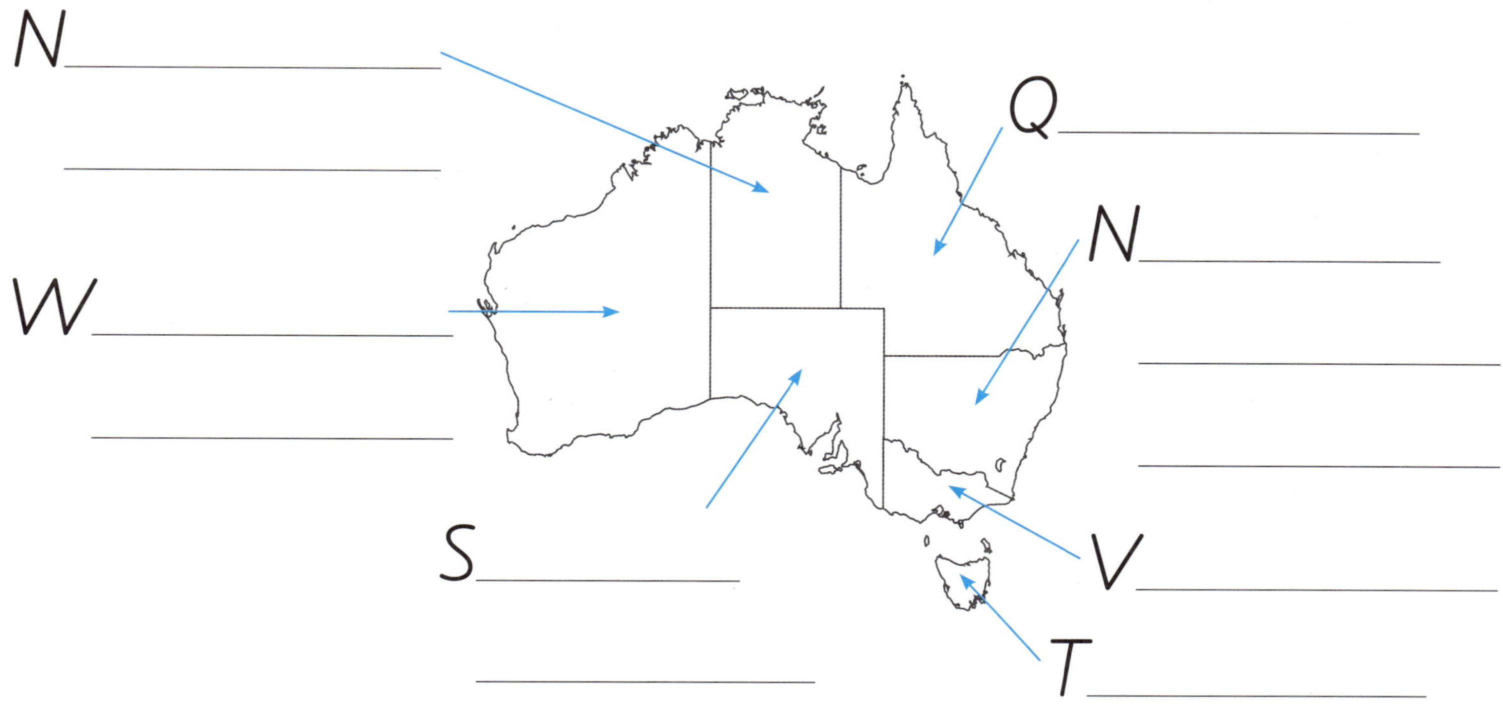

Label the planets in our solar system. Fill in the missing letters, using your knowledge from this book to help you.

Building fluency

Practise writing these words three times each.

first

team

know

ride

time

amazing

fast

people

flying

watch

walking

awesome

beautiful

Word play

Complete the word search. Words can go upwards, downwards and across. When you've found all the words, colour in the letters that are left over.

S	O	C	S	O	L	A	R	B	D	E	M	F
T	R	D	T	E	A	R	F	D	S	T	O	J
C	P	L	A	N	E	T	V	S	H	E	O	K
O	F	R	R	L	E	R	T	W	Q	S	N	Y
N	S	U	R	N	D	F	R	A	D	X	V	S
E	A	R	T	H	P	E	T	C	G	O	R	T
Q	T	R	I	N	G	S	Y	O	R	B	I	T
L	L	C	G	H	J	T	H	M	A	H	E	S
R	O	C	K	E	T	F	S	E	V	N	B	S
V	R	E	S	R	T	W	F	T	I	H	T	U
C	O	N	S	T	E	L	L	A	T	I	O	N
O	P	B	D	S	S	C	O	N	Y	R	I	N

solar star planet constellation

gravity orbit Earth Sun

Moon rings rocket comet

Independent writing

Choose a planet to conduct some research on. On the next page, complete the fact file on your planet.

Print the name of your planet.

Draw your planet.

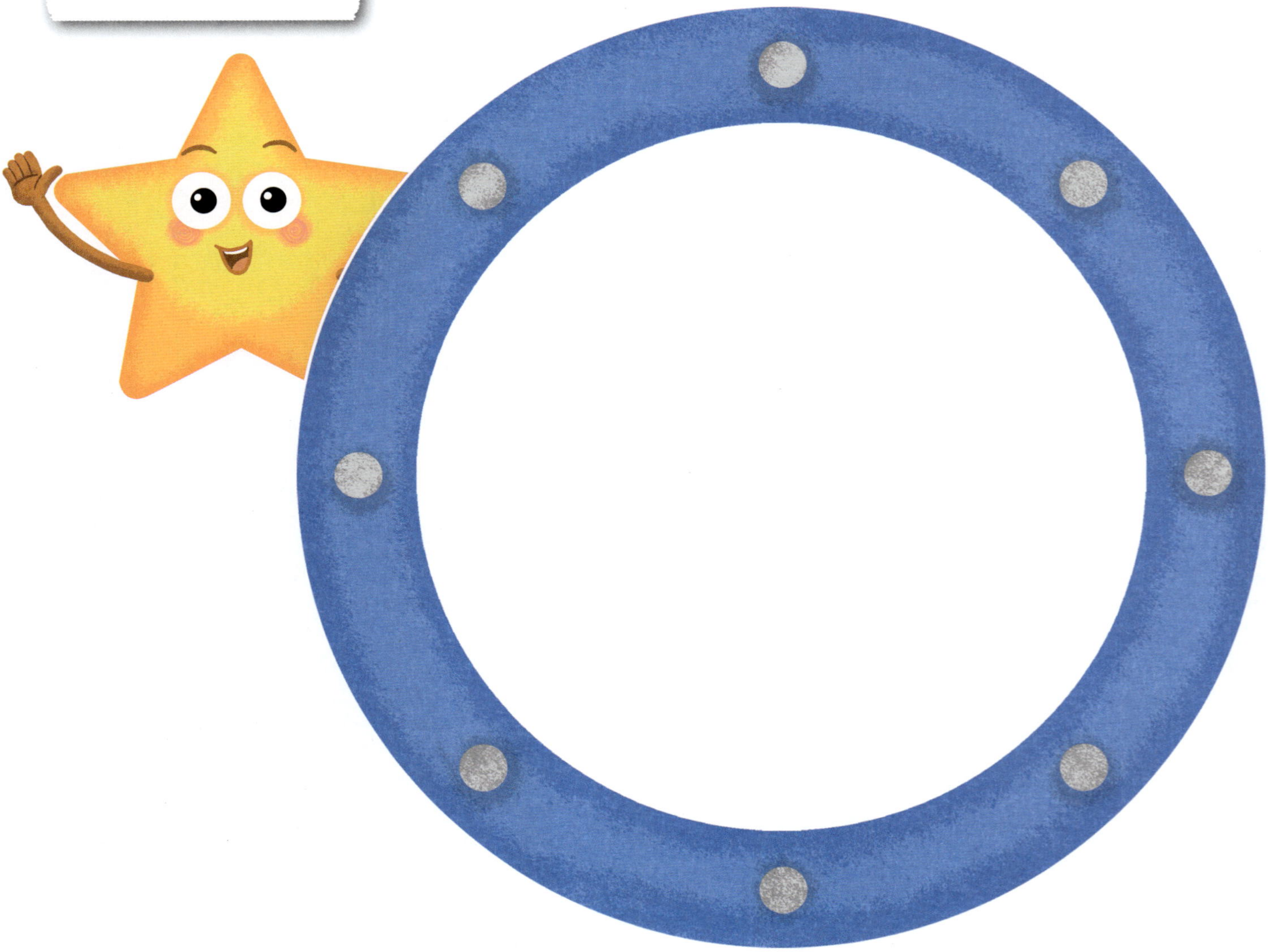

My planet fact file

Assessment: Fluency and legibility

Copy these sentences in your best cursive handwriting.

The biggest planet in the solar system is Jupiter. Jupiter is twice as massive as all the other planets combined.

Self-assessment of fluency and legibility:

Congratulations! You've learnt how to write legibly and with fluency. *Go to page 3 to complete your passport.*

- ☐ *I need more confidence*

- ☐ *I understand but need practice*

- ☐ *Over the Moon!*

I hope you had fun and improved your writing on this journey.

Teacher comment